I0002966

Companies and Communities

Participating without being sleazy

Dawn M. Foster

fastwonderblog.com

Companies and Communities
Participating without being sleazy
by
Dawn M. Foster

© 2009 Fast Wonder LLC

All Rights Reserved
including the right to reproduce or redistribute this book

Additional copies / formats of this book can be purchased at
http://fastwonderblog.com/eBooks

Published by Fast Wonder LLC
4110 SE Hawthorne #131
Portland, OR 97214

Table of Contents

Introduction

While some companies struggle with how to participate in online communities and social media, other companies take to it naturally and create an online presence that is genuinely participative and community oriented. There are right and wrong ways to interact with any online community whether it takes the form of blog comments, discussion forums, wikis, social networking, or some other mechanism. It is worth taking the time to do some research and plan for how you want to approach your community activities. This book is designed for those companies who need a little help interacting with online communities. I hope it will help you get started in way that will be productive and engaging both for your company and your community.

Definitions

I want to start with a couple of definitions of what I mean by a few of the terms used throughout this book. Most of these concepts are a bit nebulous, and each person seems to define them a little differently with conflicting ideas about what each really mean. As a result, these are not meant to be definitive industry definitions; they are simply guidelines and starting points to help people understand the basic concepts in the context of this book.

Online Community

An online environment where a group of people with similar goals or interests share experiences and build relationships using web tools.

Social Networking

Connecting with a community of people in your network through services like Facebook and Twitter with various methods of online interaction.

Social Media or New Media

Online media like blogs, podcasts, videos, and news with a strong participatory element through comments, ratings, or other mechanisms. Social media is generated by the people and for the people with content created by anyone with a voice (average Joes, village idiots, respected journalists, CxOs, …). I also consider online communities and social networking to be a subset of the broader topic of social media.

Benefits of Community

There are many reasons for a company to have an online community, but I think that the benefits can be grouped into four primary benefits.

People

Communities first & foremost are about the people. Having a community gives people a place to engage with your company. These people will talk about you and your products in blogs and other online forums whether you choose to participate or not, so giving people a place to talk about you can help you keep engaged with the conversations.

Product Innovation

Communities provide a great forum for getting product feedback. It gives you a central place to ask questions about how people use your products. You also get to see first-hand what they complain about, what issues they have, and where they have questions about you or your products.

Evangelism

Communities also help you grow evangelists for your products from outside of your company. These are the customers or users of your products that are passionate and deeply engaged with you. Interestingly enough, these people frequently come to your defense within the community when people say negative things about your company. They can also have exceptional feedback for you, so it is important to identify these people early and encourage them to get deeply engaged (often with some special community permissions). For Jivespace, I created a special "Friends of Jivespace" blog with top community members as authors.

Brand Loyalty

Having a community can also help drive brand loyalty for your products. Giving people a place to engage with you can drive a tremendous amount of loyalty for your products.

Building a Community is Like Hosting a Party

This analogy comes from Josh Bancroft, and it was such a great way to describe acceptable behavior in communities that I had to include it in this book. The idea is that as the host of a party (or a community), you provide the location, invite people to attend, encourage interesting conversations, and take care of any issues or unruly attendees. You would never try to tell people what they can talk about, kick them out of the party for offering a differing viewpoint, impose arbitrary and annoying rules, or spend the entire party talking only about yourself, yet for some reason certain people think this is an acceptable way to host a community. In other words, host your community the way you would host a party.

Josh describes the comparison from the perspective of companies who host the community or the party; however, the analogy applies equally to the people attending the party. Would you attend a party hosted by someone you dislike and spend the entire party talking about how much they suck? Would you go to a party and talk about how your house is so much better than their house? Would you spend the evening lying to people? Would you spend all night talking about yourself without listening to any of the other participant? I'm going to guess that the answer to these questions is 'no' at least for most of us. You should not expect to participate in a community using these types of behaviors. Be a good host and a well behaved participant at parties and in communities. The guiding principles in the next section and other sections in this book will provide more information about what is and is not acceptable behavior within online communities whether you are hosting the community or participating as a member.

Guiding Principles

There are some basic guiding principles that should be used to guide community participation within a company or other organization. These should apply to participation in most online social media environments, including online communities and social networks, but they are not meant to be a rule book. As you participate in online social environments, you should be thinking about these guidelines and finding the right way to apply them in your situation. Participating within the spirit of these principles is more important than memorizing them and applying them in a black or white, all or nothing approach. Anything involving real people comes in shades of gray, and these guidelines are no different.

Social Principles

Be Sincere

Sincerity is a critical element; if you aren't able to be sincere, then social media is probably not the best medium for you. Being sincere in your social communications will increase your credibility, and if you appear to be simply going through the motions, people are unlikely to waste their attention on your messages. Sincerity goes a long way toward believability and credibility.

Focus on the individuals

Participation in online communities and social media should be focused on the individuals, not the corporate entity. For example, it is OK to have group blogs for a company as long as posts are tied to individuals (real people), but you wouldn't want to have a blog where every post is authored by "company name" or "admin". People work at companies, but the real connections and networks happen between individuals. Show a little personality and little bit of who you are from a personal standpoint.

Not all about you

Social media is a conversation, which is by definition two-way. In other words, it is not all about you, your company, your products or your agenda. It involves listening and participating in the broader community of people. Don't just expect people to help you; jump in and help other people in areas where you have some expertise. If all you do is pimp your products without adding to the broader conversation, people will lose interest in you pretty quickly.

Be a Part of the Community

Just talking *at* people isn't going to cut it in this new social world where the community is critical. You should be a part of the broader community of people with similar interests both online and offline by participating in, but not trying to control the community. Engaging in conversations and when possible actually meeting those people who comment on your content, follow you on Twitter, or friend you on Facebook can go a long way toward making real, lasting connections with people. Attend local meetups, comment on content from people who read your content, engage in online discussion forums, and engage in other places where you can find people from your community of peers.

Everyone's a Peer

The days of expert speakers who talk at us while we passively absorb the information with little or no opportunity for discussion are gradually disappearing. This is the old media model: unreachable experts are on TV, the radio, and in print. Now, anyone can publish video, audio podcasts, and online writing while commenting on the content produced by others. Granted, not all of it will be professional quality; however, with an open mind, I think you might be surprised at all of the opportunities to learn from others. We each come into a discussion with unique and diverse ideas, and we learn by listening and sharing ideas with our peers aka everyone.

Participation

You don't need to participate in everything, especially to start. As a matter of fact, I would discourage participating in too many at once. Jump in with one idea to start, try it for a while, learn and build on it. I would recommend starting with Twitter or blogging. After you get a feel for what works and what doesn't for you, pick and choose a few more that make sense for you. I'll introduce the major elements here and then elaborate on them in future chapters.

Blogging

I recommend having both a personal blog and a company blog. I tend to like company group blogs, especially for small companies, where several people from the company regularly blog about various topics related to the company. The key is not to use your corporate blog only to pimp your products or for press releases. You should be talking about your industry and sharing your thoughts on the broader market as a whole in addition to talking about your products. Become a thought leader in your industry through your blog. Likewise, your personal blog shouldn't be all about your company. It's fine to talk about your company (the reality is that we spend most of our waking hours at work); however, this is your personal blog. Branch out a little. Talk about your other passions, especially the ones tangentially related to your work. Make sure your blog contains a blogroll linking to other bloggers you respect; not to have one is really bad form (see the above section: Not all about You).

Twitter

Twitter is a way to send short format (140 character) messages to a bunch of people while also reading messages from others. People have mixed reactions to Twitter, but I think that Twitter is only as interesting as the people you follow. If you follow people with interesting things to say, you will probably get more out of the experience. Talk about interesting things (personal and professional), engage in conversations, interact with other people, follow friends and industry luminaries, and have some fun with it. Feel free to talk about your products, link to your blog posts, and talk about what you are working on, but if all you do is pimp your stuff, people are unlikely to follow your posts (again, it is not all about you).

Audio and Video Podcasting

Podcasting is a great way to distribute content that doesn't fit as well into written form. Audio podcasts are really good for interviews to talk to other experts or to record interesting discussions that happen as part of conference panels. I have done a few Fast Wonder podcasts as interviews with interesting people doing cool things in communities or as recordings of round table discussions. Video is great for demonstrations or presentations where you want to show people something. Screencasts with voice-overs work particularly well, especially for technical topics or marketing videos. While I was working at Jive Software, I worked with the developers to do screencasts and other videos fairly regularly for the Jivespace Developer Community.

Facebook

You may be noticing a trend here, but your Facebook "presence" should be focused on individuals: people within your company, especially your executives, sharing information. Like with Twitter, people should create accounts and share some personal information along with the corporate information. If you want to have a "corporate presence" on Facebook, do it as a group that people can join or a page where people can be a "fan of" your company, not a company profile masquerading as a person.

Other Social Networks

For companies trying to reach out to a younger crowd, MySpace might be a better choice than Facebook. You can also find niche social networks for many different groups or demographics from technology specific communities to weight loss to politics to anything else you can imagine. Find the ones that apply to you and use the guidelines above along with some initial lurking around the community to come up with the best ways to participate.

Industry Communities

Many industries have communities for people who work in a specific field or who are passionate about an industry topic (PCWorld is one example in the technology industry). In these communities make sure that the people participating are the subject matter experts in their field, rather than public relations, sales, or marketing (unless the community is specifically focused on one of those groups). Find the people that are already passionate about the topic and have them participate as part of their job.

Custom Communities for Your Company

There are also some very good reasons to create a new community focused on your customers or your industry, but again it isn't all about you. A good way to think about corporate communities is that the community "owns" the community . The company owns the infrastructure, facilitates the discussions, moderates and keeps people in check without being too heavy handed. Again, it isn't all about you, so be careful not to constantly spam the community with your marketing messages. If the company doesn't play nice with the community, the community will take discussions elsewhere.

Many More

The ways to participate listed above are what I would consider the basics right now. However, there are many, many more ways to engage with your community: Second Life, discussion boards / community sites, Ning, Flickr, meetups and events, and more. In short, go to those places that make sense for your company. If the industry thought leaders in your market are participating in a social networking site, it is likely that you should also be engaging in conversations there.

As I said earlier, any one company does not necessarily need to participate everywhere. Use your best judgment and participate

© 2009 Fast Wonder LLC

in ways that make sense for your company.

© 2009 Fast Wonder LLC

Blogs and Blogging

We are finally moving past the era where people thought of blogs as a consumer phenomenon, where discussions focused on kids, pets, weekend excursions, and other personal topics rather than serious corporate content. However, many companies have not ventured into blogging, yet.

Corporate Blogs are Important

The research shows that more people are reading blogs, those people expect your company to have a social media presence, and blogs influence their purchasing decisions. Those sound like very compelling reasons for companies to start blogging or to improve their existing blog.

The Research

Cone Finds that Americans Expect Companies to Have a Presence in Social Media: September 25, 2008

"Sixty percent of Americans use social media, and of those, 59 percent interact with companies on social media Web sites. One in four interacts more than once per week.

According to the survey, 93 percent of social media users believe a company should have a presence in social media, while an overwhelming 85 percent believe a company should not only be present but also interact with its consumers via social media. In fact, 56 percent of users feel both a stronger connection with and better served by companies when they can interact with them in a social media environment.

"The news here is that Americans are eager to deepen their brand relationships through social media," explains Mike Hollywood, director of new media for Cone, "it isn't an intrusion into their lives, but rather a welcome channel for discussion." (Quoted from Cone: September 25, 2008)

Forrester Research: The Growth Of Social Technology Adoption on October 20, 2008

"One in three online Americans now read blogs at least once a month, while 18% comment on them. Blog readers as a group grew by nearly 50% over this past year. (Quoted from Forrester Research: October 20, 2008)

BuzzLogic: Blog Influence on Consumer Purchases Eclipses Social Networks on October 28, 2008

"Blogs influence purchases: One half (50 percent) of blog readers say they find blogs useful for purchase information.

According to the study, blogs factor in to critical stages of the purchase process, weighing most heavily at the actual moment of a purchase decision. When it comes to respondents who said they have trusted blog content for purchase decisions in the past, over half (52 percent) say blogs played a role in the critical moment they decided to move forward with a purchase. (Quoted from BuzzLogic: October 28, 2008)

What This Means for Companies

For those of us who regularly consume information from blogs, we expect to be able to grab an RSS feed of your company's blog to keep up with news and information relevant to your industry. The research above shows that the number of people who read blogs is growing, and these people expect you to have a blog. Not only are **more people reading blogs**, these blogs are **influencing purchasing decisions**, which is important for every company.

Additional Benefits of Blogging

Search Engine Optimization (SEO). SEO is probably one of the biggest advantages of having a corporate blog. Because blog content is updated frequently, blogs have some built-in search engine benefits. The blogging culture also encourages linking to other blogs, which can also improve your rankings in search results.

Thought leadership. A great blog can position your company and key employees as thought leaders within the industry, which puts your company in a position of greater authority within your industry. The O'Reilly Radar blog is a great example of how O'Reilly employees and the company are seen as thought leaders, thus putting O'Reilly in a greater position of authority for books, events, and other products.

Strategy and Vision

Blogs are still just another piece of the corporate communications puzzle (although an increasingly important piece), so spending some quality time thinking about what you want to achieve with your overall communication strategy and how blogging fits into that strategy is a good place for companies to start. You don't want to use your blog to just pimp your products or talk about press releases. A blog can be used for so much more. Think about the areas where you want to lead the industry and the topics that you want people to think about when they think of your company. Use your blog to become a thought leader in the industry by sharing your expertise on those broad topics that are important and relevant to your company.

Think about who should be blogging on your corporate blog. It is easy to pick your top 5 executives, and give them access to the blog. In some cases, they might be the perfect people, but they aren't always the best choice when it comes to accomplishing your goals for the blog. Go back to your discussion about your strategy for the blog and the topics that you want people to think about when they think of your company or your products. Who in your company has expertise in those areas? Do you have someone with great ideas? Are there any evangelists or other employees passionate about those topics? If so, recruit those people to contribute to your blogs. Someone passionate and smart, but outside of the senior management ranks probably has more time to spend on the blog and might just come up with some innovative and interesting ideas.

You should also branch out a little into the realm of unofficial or personal blogs. Encourage your employees to have their own blogs (personal in the sense of owned by a person, not the company) where they talk about their areas of expertise. I have blogged on various corporate blogs for companies and non-profit organizations that I am associated with, but I also continue to blog at Fast Wonder on various topics related to social media, online communities, and other technology topics. Having a personal blog has a number of benefits, including giving us an excuse to learn and research new ideas. Quite a few people have similar blogs, and I like to believe that some people think that we have interesting things to say and that our companies benefit from having smart people discussing their expertise outside of official work channels. There is also a caution to go along with this. You don't want to create a personal blog that is too focused on your company. If all you talk about is your company and you cover all of the same topics as your official blog, it just looks forced and insincere. You need to branch out and cover additional topics; show that you are a real person and not just a corporate shill.

Making it Happen

After the initial excitement wears off, it is easy for companies to neglect the corporate blog. We just forget to blog, and before long, no one has posted in a month (or two or three …) In some companies this isn't a problem. If you already have a bunch of prolific bloggers neglect may not be an issue, but for the rest of you, and you know who you are, it really helps to have someone "in charge" of the blog. This person isn't responsible for writing all of the content, but they can be responsible for herding and nagging in addition to making sure that some specific strategic topics are being addressed on the blog. The role is part strategist and part mother hen (it isn't all that different from managing communities), so you have to find someone who can think strategically about your industry and the right topics while they follow up obsessively to make sure people are actually posting to the blog.

Content is King

Many corporate blogs are neglected, dull, and unimaginative while filled with press release content, marketing fluff, and old content. However, it doesn't have to be this way. Corporate blogs can be interesting and useful with a little focus and time devoted to it. Here are a few tips to help turn your boring corporate blog into something successful.

Content Roadmap

Most companies should create and maintain some type of content roadmap. The content roadmap will usually map out the next 4 weeks of blog posts with an author identified for each post. This helps to ensure that the blog topics are strategically aligned with corporate goals, varied across topics and types of content, and frequent enough to keep the blog active. The person responsible for the blog can work with authors to help identify topics and then make sure that the author has access to everything needed to complete the post (data, technical assistance, etc.)

Spontaneous Posts

Now that you have a content roadmap, you should also diverge from it frequently to allow for serendipitous blogging on hot topics or new ideas that people are passionate enough about to want to talk about them immediately. Monitor popular blogs, news sources, and events in your industry and respond to what others are saying. Join the conversation without waiting for the topic to come up on the content roadmap.

Thought Leadership

The best blogs have content that focuses on thought leadership. Blog about the things in your industry where your employees have expertise that can be shared with the world. Don't just talk about your products; focus on your entire industry. Get people to discuss a variety of topics and new ideas. Don't get stuck in a rut where all of your posts have essentially the same or similar content. You are not a thought leader if all of your posts are simply variations on a single idea. Chime in with your thoughts on a variety of topics across your industry.

Conversations

Always monitor and respond to comments on your blog. People get frustrated with blogs where people ask questions or provide feedback in the comments without any response or acknowledgement. Even worse are those companies that moderate every comment and delete anything that they do not agree with. Let people comment and disagree with your ideas. Some of the most interesting conversations happen in the comments of a blog post. You should also monitor what people are saying about you on other blogs, forums, Twitter, etc. and respond where appropriate. There is a whole section on monitoring dashboards later in the book.

Blogs are Fun

Have fun with your blog, and don't be so serious all of the time. You can include interesting things that are happening within your company that aren't necessarily work related (photos from a company ski trip). Admit it; you would rather read a blog post with great content and some humor mixed in, instead of something with great content that drones on and on like an old, boring college lecture. Make the content interesting and fun enough that people will look forward to reading your posts.

Communication Issues on Corporate Blogs

Managing communications can be easier when you have a single company blog with fewer authors. It can get very tricky when managing corporate communications for a company the size of Microsoft or Intel with many blogs and many people communicating with the outside world.

Many companies use their blogs as a way to make announcements and other official communications for the outside world. For your readers, it can be difficult to know whether a blog post is an official announcement or something less formal. In companies, like Microsoft, with bloggers spanning across many blogs, it can help to educate people to clearly state whether something is opinion or an official statement. When I worked at Intel, my intel.com blog and my Fast Wonder blog had disclaimers at the top of the sidebar making it clear that the posts were my opinions and not official statements. It can also help to educate bloggers about including clarification within the text of certain types of posts. We get so wrapped up in our work that we don't always take the time to think about how our actions will be perceived by people outside of the company, but it can help to give bloggers a little training to help them learn how to create better blog posts rather than focusing on damage control later. Lightweight social media guidelines might also help in some situations.

I suspect that this is mainly an issue for larger companies or

© 2009 Fast Wonder LLC

ones that tightly control communications. I've worked at several smaller companies where this issue never came up at all. In other words, don't sweat the communications issues unless you really think that it might be an issue at your company.

A few tips for managing communications
- Include disclaimers in the sidebars for blogs that contain opinions and not official statements.
- Clarify whether a blog post is an announcement or something less official if readers might be confused.
- Train bloggers to think about how their posts might be perceived by those outside the company.
- Put a very lightweight set of social media guidelines in place designed to help people, not prevent them from posting (guidelines, not rules).

Examples of Good Corporate Blogs

There are a few companies that do a good job of corporate blogging from a content perspective.

Vidoop

Many different employees pitch in on the Vidoop corporate blog (not just the execs) to talk about a wide variety of topics. You'll find some very interesting perspectives and thoughts about their industry (OpenID, identity, etc.) mixed in with links to important industry news, interviews, new features, announcements, site maintenance, and more. One of the more interesting topics they covered is a series of posts describing their move from Tulsa, OK to Portland, OR.

Google

While this blog has a lot of posts that look like they could be press releases for new products, most of them don't read like press releases. Google has a pretty good mix of product pieces along with general information (keeping kids safe online, fighting spam, etc.) and a few fun posts about activities that Googlers participate in.

Southwest

Along with announcements about when booking opens for the winter holiday flights, the Southwest blog talks about environmental concerns, awards, burgers, beer, and water balloons.

Zappos

This is probably one of the most fun corporate blogs I've seen in a while. They talk about the origin of French heels, running tips, history of the penny loafer, baby quail, rock band, Mexican food, and much more.

Tripwire

Tripwire's Virtual Security and Virtual Black Hole blogs are a wealth of information about virtualization trends and best practices. What could be more dreadfully dull than a blog about virtualization? Yet, they manage to present relevant information while drawing comparisons to Jedi mind tricks and Yosemite Sam. Any blog that can make virtualization and security interesting is worth the time to read.

Details are Critical

While the content of the posts is the most important part of the blog, do not neglect the other little details that can make a difference. There are a few additional elements that make a blog different from other parts of your website. These are all important, so make sure that someone is spending the time needed to make sure that they are included in a way that is appropriate for your corporate blog.

Blogroll

Make sure your blog contains a blogroll linking to other bloggers you respect; not to have one is really bad form (refer back to the guidelines: not all about you). Link to the people that you read, the other thought leaders in your industry, and other blogs that your employees write in your blogroll. This goes for your personal / unofficial blogs, too. All blogs should have one, and if you don't want to put it in a sidebar, you can create a separate page devoted to your blogroll.

Sidebars

Spend some quality time thinking about your sidebars. Add items that make it easy for people to find older content on your blog: search, tag cloud, recent posts, popular posts, etc. Don't forget to include links back to other key parts of your website including information about products, press releases or other news, and events where people can find you. Include some fun stuff in the sidebar, too (Flickr photos, twitter posts, etc.) Don't let your sidebars get too cluttered, but do make sure that you include helpful, relevant, and interesting content in them.

Analytics

You will want to know how many people read your blog, and exactly what they are most interested in reading. Make sure that you install some kind of analytics package; for example, Google Analytics is free and easy to embed. This will tell you where your visitors came from and which posts they are reading. You can use this information to determine what people are most interested in.

RSS Feeds

Don't forget to also pay attention to your RSS feeds for those people seeing your content in RSS readers. Do not use your blogging tool's default RSS feeds as your primary blog feeds. Always run them through a service that provides more information and statistics about who is reading your blog. Google's Feedburner is a great (and free) tool to get more information about the people subscribing to your feeds, and it provides an easy way for you to allow people to subscribe by email.

Should Every Company Have a Blog?

Yes and no. The benefits of blogging seem to be fairly clear; however, these benefits are only achieved when the blog is updated regularly with great content. Unfortunately, this can be a significant time commitment. For companies who are not willing to put in the time and effort, it is better not to have a blog than to have a blog that hasn't been updated in months.

Here are a few things to think about:
- Can you commit to at least one post per week? (2-3 is better)
- Do you have people who have interesting things to say and with good writing skills?
- Is someone available to manage the process and make sure that the blog never gets neglected?

If the answer to any of the above questions is no, this might not be the right time for you to start a corporate blog.

Making it easier

There are a few tricks to help overcome the hurdles when starting a corporate blog.

Group blogs. Start a group blog with several authors to spread the load across more people. With 4 authors, each person could write one post a month to meet the minimum requirement of one post per week. A dozen authors writing 2 posts per month would give you content for a post each business day.

Recruit great people. Recruit bloggers from the lower ranks of the company who are smart and passionate about the industry. While the CEO might not have hours to spend blogging, someone further down the org chart might be able to carve out a little more time.

Manage the process. Manage the blog process by having someone who already manages content for other purposes also pick up management of the blog. A community manager is a good choice for this if you have one.

Corporate blogging is a complex topic, and there will never be one magic formula that applies to all companies. Hopefully, these tips will help a few people make their corporate blogs even better. Keep in mind that you will make mistakes along the way. Learn from them, keep writing, and continue to make incremental improvements.

With a little effort, you can have a successful corporate blog. It just takes focus, dedication and resources; however, the payoff in search engine optimization and thought leadership in your industry is well worth the time and effort to put together a great corporate blog.

Twitter

You should think of Twitter as one more way to engage with the people in your community. The Twitter demographic skews a little higher in age than many social sites with a large number of users in their 30's and 40's. It is also popular with the technology and early adopter crowd, so it is an application that should be taken seriously despite the detractors who think it is only good for learning what your friends are eating for dinner.

While the original intent of Twitter was to answer the question, "what are you doing?" in 140 characters or less, people are using it for so much more. We ask questions and get recommendations while responding to similar requests from our friends. Sharing of news, information, upcoming events, and links to interesting content are also popular activities on Twitter.

How does it work?

On the surface, Twitter is simple. You get 140 characters to send an update.

Getting Started

To get started, you just need to create an account on Twitter; however, don't stop with creating the account. Here are a few things you should do before you really get started:

- add a picture or an avatar that helps people recognize you
- spend a few minutes on your bio to help people learn a little more about you
- post a few quick updates. Hint: the first one should not talk about how you are starting to use Twitter – that will be obvious. Share a link, talk about a topic, or say something interesting.

Now that you have a few introductory tweets, you can start adding a few friends. Don't go overboard on this step – pick and choose carefully! Start with no more than 25 people, preferably people that you already know. If this is a corporate account, be especially careful. Many people feel strange about brands following them out of the blue. For corporate accounts, follow a few employees or close friends to start with and let other people find you (see the Best Practices section below for more suggestions on following).

I also recommend that people who are new to Twitter try a couple of the desktop clients. I've found that using a Twitter client helps me be much more productive with Twitter. I like Tweetdeck because it allows you to group followers and set up constant searches, but Twhirl is great if you are managing multiple Twitter accounts. You can try a few clients before you settle on the one you like best.

The Language of Twitter

Twitter can seem very foreign until you learn to translate between Twitter speak and the English language.

Here are a few shortcuts that you need to know:

- @reply: A way to reply to someone publicly on Twitter. Example: "@geekygirldawn thanks for sending me the link."
- Direct Message: A way to reply to someone privately on Twitter. In general, most discussions should be public, but this is a good way to send sensitive data. Example: "d geekygirldawn you can call me on my cell phone at 555-867-5309."
- OH: Stands for overheard and is not usually attributed to a specific person. These are usually humorous. Example: "OH: I took shop class and didn't lose any fingers. I bet I could use a chainsaw"
- RT: Retweets are a way to re-send something from another Twitter user to your followers while attributing it to the original author. Example: "RT @geekygirldawn: Don't forget to RSVP for BarCampPortland!"
- #: Hashtags are used to tag Twitter posts. Example: "The bubble tea has arrived. #barcampportland"

Best Practices

While the premise of Twitter is very simple, not unlike many social environments there are some nuances, expectations and ways to behave. This is especially true for corporations participating on Twitter, so here are a few best practices designed to make sure that you participate in a way that helps, rather than hinders, your efforts.

Know what people are saying about you

After you create your Twitter account and have the name reserved, but before you start using it, set up some tracking tools. You will want to know when people are replying and what people are saying about you on Twitter. Twitter search and Yahoo Pipes are both good places to start. You will find many more details about how to track and monitor conversations in the Monitoring Dashboards section of this book. I monitor the RSS feeds most of the day when I have time, but no less than 2-3 times per day.

Respond frequently and sincerely

Knowing what people say is only helpful if you actually use the information and respond to people. You will want to keep the responses public by using @replies wherever possible instead of DMs unless you are exchanging non-public information.

Going back to the Guiding Principles section earlier in this book, you also need to be sincere and remember that it is not all about you when you respond to people. Be honest about what isn't working well and how you plan to improve your products or services. Help people find information when you see them struggling or asking questions on Twitter. Respond to the tough, critical questions in addition to the easy ones.

Follow back

You will want to follow people back when they follow you on Twitter. It will help you listen and respond while allowing people to send you direct messages. Following back is also considered good Twitter etiquette, especially for companies. A quick email to the Twitter support team can help manage this process by converting your account to one that automatically follows anyone who chooses to follow you. I've done this for a couple of corporate accounts and accounts used with local events. Please see the Don't Proactively Follow People' section below for some cautions about following people.

Have a personality

You've heard this before, but please keep in mind that companies are made up of people, and you'll want to show some personality in your tweets. Nobody wants to listen to a corporate drone or regurgitated marketing messages. Personalize the information and act like a real person in your responses. Don't be afraid to let your followers know more about the person or people behind the Twitter account.

Variety is Important

Include a wide variety of information in your Twitter stream without focusing too heavily on any one element. I try to shoot for a mix of informational posts (new features, blog posts), links to other people's blog posts or retweets, @replies to questions, alerts about any issues or downtime for maintenance, meetups, and fun posts.

Things to Avoid

In addition to the best practices, there are also plenty of behaviors that you will want to avoid. Most of these will result in a loss of followers and a general lack of respect for your organization. Stick to the Best Practices above and avoid these slimy practices.

Don't be a link spam account

This one is a little controversial, and some people will disagree with me here; however, I don't think that you should use your Twitter account just to post links to blog posts. If people want your blog posts, they can get them via RSS. It is OK to link to informational blog posts, but I always put some text around it so that people can decide whether or not to click through. You should also be linking to posts from other blogs that are relevant to your company or industry as a whole. These should be a fairly small portion of your overall Twitter posts (see the variety is important section above).

Don't go overboard

You should be providing information and replying to people, but you shouldn't go overboard. I would say that posting no more than 5-10 times a day on average is a pretty good goal. Some days will have more and others less depending on the situation; however, if you post too much, you'll start to lose followers who can't keep up with the volume.

Don't be too self-promotional

You should use your Twitter account to promote your activities; however, it should be a part of what you do. If every post talks about how awesome your company is, people will lose interest fairly quickly.

Don't promote anything via direct messages

Using direct messages to promote your blog posts or other activities is the equivalent of email spam, but about 100 times worse, since these are delivered to many people over SMS messages. I suggest never promoting anything to people using direct messages. You can use direct messages to follow up with someone who was having an issue, but even in those cases, I would use it very sparingly.

Don't proactively follow people

People will find your Twitter account when you @reply them, and you can use your website / blog to promote it. You don't want to start by following a few hundred (or thousand) people who don't care about you or your product. It seems creepy to be followed by a random brand that you aren't already following, and it just makes you look spammy. See the follow back section above for how to do this right.

Twitter can be a great way to reach out and connect with people who are interested in your company or your products. Just be careful about how you participate and adhere to these few simple guidelines if you want to be successful using Twitter for your brand.

© 2009 Fast Wonder LLC

Social Networks

Social networks can be an important part of any community strategy both from the standpoint of reaching your audience and because you can use social networks as a place to host a community. No one social network is perfect for every use. The key is to find the social network that meets your needs and fits with your audience.

Please note that my analysis skews heavily toward what I see working with clients based in United States. The interesting thing about social networks is that they tend to be regional with certain sites being much more or less popular in certain countries. In this section, I am only going to cover the top few social networks that seem to have quite a bit of usage globally and in the United States with examples of how they can be used, but you will need to do some research on your audience to determine which social networks will be right for your needs.

Facebook

Facebook is probably the social network that has the broadest audience and the most community functionality of any of the big services right now. One of the reasons that I find Facebook so interesting is because it has a variety of features that are focused on community building and sharing information with friends and contacts. It is especially useful for smaller, lightweight community efforts.

While we tend to think of Facebook as something for college students, recent college graduates, and technology early adopters, the reality is that Facebook users in the 35 and older category are growing at a very fast rate. According to Inside Facebook, as of the end of March, 30% of Facebook users are over 35 with the following breakdown:

- 13 – 17 years: 11%
- 18 – 25 years: 35%
- 26 – 34 years: 24%
- 35 – 44 years: 17%
- 45 – 54 years: 8%
- 55 – 65 years: 5%

There are several primary ways to participate on Facebook: personal profiles (private), pages (public), groups, and applications. Each one of these is used differently, so I'll cover each one of them individually.

Personal Profiles (Private)

This is where you should start on Facebook, whether you are participating for fun or on behalf of a company. Facebook profiles are private by default - only the people that you add as contacts can view your personal profile, and they are designed to be used by individuals. You will use this as your account to log into Facebook, so you should work on building your personal profile before starting any other efforts on Facebook. This also gives you an opportunity to experiment with Facebook to learn what works for you and what doesn't while participating as an individual, rather than jeopardizing your corporate brand image with costly mistakes and gaffes.

Here are a few things that you can do to get started:

- Add a picture that helps people recognize you. There are many other people named Dawn Foster, so it is important for people to be able to tell for certain that they are looking at your account instead of a stranger with a similar name.
- Spend a few minutes entering your information (personal info, education / work, etc.)
- Post status updates and add a few extra pictures.
- Add a few friends (personal, work, past lives)
- Try to get a mix of personal and professional information to help people better understand the whole you with as much information as you feel comfortable sharing with people.
- Go easy on your friends – save the poking, zombie requests, etc. for close personal friends.

Please do not create a personal profile for your company. These look weird and artificial, and they are designed to be private, which makes it difficult for people to interact with your company. We'll talk about better ways to have a company presence on Facebook in the next section.

Pages (Public)

Facebook pages are publicly viewable, which makes them much better for a corporate presence, since anyone can become a fan of your company without any additional interaction or approvals. People are effectively using pages for companies, products, bands, shows, special interest groups, and much more. Facebook pages have many of the same features as profile pages, but with information that is geared toward companies rather than individuals. While profile pages have education / work information and interests, public pages have location, hours of operation, company overview, mission, date founded, and more. Some features include: wall with messages, events, video, pictures, notes, and more.

Groups

Groups are usually used to share information, collaborate or organize around a specific topic, and they can be public or private depending on what you want to achieve from the group. Groups can be a way to create a very simple, lightweight community around an effort, especially if most of your audience is already on Facebook. People can become members by joining the group, and then they can post information to the group. The features are similar to the profiles and pages described above with information, wall / discussions, events, photos, links, video and more.

Applications

You might consider creating an application for your organization as a way for people to interact with your products. For example, companies like Nike and Intel have created Facebook applications.

Be cautious when using applications. Some applications have been linked to viruses and others spam all of your contacts in order to use the application. However, there are some great uses of applications. I use the Twitter application to feed my Twitter status to Facebook, and I use the Upcoming application to display a list of events that I'm attending. As I mentioned earlier, go easy on your friends – save the applications used for poking, zombie requests, etc. for close personal friends, not business acquaintences.

There are certainly other ways to use Facebook, but this covers the basic ways that most people use it. In general, remember to participate as a person first and a company second, and remember that the guiding principles that I have talked in previous sections also apply to using Facebook.

MySpace

If you are trying to reach a younger audience (teens and 20s) or if you are in the music industry, then you might want to use MySpace. While MySpace is a good way to reach certain groups of people, their community features are lacking. Unlike Facebook, you won't be able to create lightweight communities on MySpace.

MySpace is also geared almost exclusively toward individuals and bands with few ways for companies to participate. Similarly to Facebook, you should start by making sure that some people in your company are on MySpace as individuals. This is the best way to learn how to use any new social network. I would start by getting a personal account, entering your personal profile information, and adding a few people that you know as friends.

Since MySpace isn't really intended for companies, I'm not going to provide any specific advice for how to create a company presence on MySpace. You should think about what you want to accomplish on MySpace and then figure out whether or not it can be accomplished within the structure of MySpace.

Niche Social Networks

While Facebook and MySpace are popular social networking sites, I strongly encourage you to look for niche social networks where you can find the specific people you want to reach within certain industries, demographics, and geographic regions.

Here are a couple of examples to help you get started:

- Orkut: popular social network for people in Brazil
- Bebo: popular social network for people in the UK
- LinkedIn: great for jobs and recruiting
- Professional associations: social networks of members
- Industries: social networks for people working in that industry
- Baby boomer and retirement: social networks for this growing segment

Finding these social networks requires some traditional market research on your specific needs. Locating your target market and the people within it online is similar to finding them in the real world. You will probably need to spend some time researching and surveying the market to find the right niche social networks for your needs.

Custom Corporate Communities

Corporate communities refer to any custom community created by an organization for the purpose of engaging with customers or other people who may be interested in the organization's products and services. For the purpose of this book, custom corporate communities include communities created by corporations, non-profit organizations, educational institutions and similar organizations. These corporate communities can take many different forms: support communities, developer communities to help developers work with your products, customer and enthusiast communities, and many others.

Getting Started and Initial Planning

Before jumping in to create a new community, you should think carefully about the purpose of this new community including your goals and objectives, fitting your community efforts into your organization's overall strategy, measuring success, and committing the resources required to make your community flourish. Here are a few questions that can help you think through the process of planning for your new community:

What is your overall strategy and how does the community fit with it?

If your custom corporate community does not support the overall strategies of the organization, I give it about a 5% chance of being successful. Creating a new community can be a very large project with quite a bit of upfront work to create the community along with a large effort over the life of the community to manage and maintain it. If this time and effort is spent in support of the overall corporate strategy, then it will be much easier to justify keeping the community during the next planning cycle for your organization. On the other hand, when a community is built to support goals that are not clearly aligned with the overall strategy, people will look at it as a big expense that can be cut, and your community will die a quick death if you are lucky or a horrible slow death by neglect if you aren't quite as fortunate.

Spend the time now to make sure that you can find a way to structure your community plans to support the overall strategy of your organization. If you can't find a good way to align your plans with the strategy, you should think twice about whether a corporate community is an appropriate solution for you right now.

What do you hope to accomplish and what are your goals for the community?

Think very carefully about why you are creating a new community for your organization. Spend plenty of time upfront to clearly define the reasons for creating it and what you will accomplish by having the community. Think back to the earlier section on the benefits of having a community. You might want to consider some or all of those benefits when you think about the goals for your community:

- *People*: gives people a place to engage with your company
- *Product Innovation*: get product feedback and ideas
- *Evangelism*: help you grow evangelists for your products from outside of your company
- *Brand Loyalty*: engagement can drive a tremendous amount of loyalty for your products

After you have a good grasp on what you hope to accomplish, you need to set some specific goals for the project. When you get into the platform selection process and design phase later in the project, having clear goals will help ensure that you build the right kind of community to achieve these goals.

What are your plans for achieving your goals and how will you measure success?

Now that you have some goals for what you want to accomplish with your community, you need to figure out the specific steps required to achieve your goals along with the metrics you will use to measure whether or not you have been successful. The metrics that you select will depend on your specific goals, but common community metrics include page views or visits, new member sign ups, and participation (new posts or replies). It is easy to go overboard and measure everything; however, I recommend that you pick a couple (no more than 4 or 5) of the most important measurements to use to report to management on your success. You should have an analytics package or reporting tools that allow you to drill down for more details that you can use to help troubleshoot issues and understand the data, but use the details as background materials for your team while focusing on the top measurements for regular tracking and management reports.

Do you need to build new or can you join an existing community?

This is the reality check portion of the process. If you can join an existing community and get the same or similar benefits for your organization without investing all of the resources to create something new, you should seriously consider joining rather than building. You should also look around your organization to see if you have any existing communities or other infrastructure that you can reuse instead of installing yet another piece of community software.

Do you have the resources (people and financing) to maintain it long-term?

As I mentioned earlier, building a new community is a big effort. It is not one of those projects that you complete and move onto the next one. Building the community and installing the software is the first step, and the real work comes in after the launch of the community. You will need to have people on board and ready to manage the day to day responsibilities from a community perspective and to administer and maintain the software. For a small community this could be a single person, but for a large corporate community, it usually takes a team of people.

You should also plan for frequent upgrades and adjustments to the community, especially right after the launch. You will find bugs in the software, areas of the community that the users find difficult to use for whatever reason, and other things you will need to adjust once you have people actually using the community. Your organization should be ready to handle these ongoing costs and resource commitments over the life of the community. Nothing is worse than wasting time and money on something that won't be maintained long enough to achieve your goals.

Now that you have thought through the issues; set your goals, objectives, and metrics; and convinced yourself and your organization that you should create this community, there are a few more implementation details to consider.

Community Ownership

Community ownership is a tricky issue. By ownership, I am not referring to legal ownership, but about something a little more abstract. I'm sure the courts would come up with a different conclusion than the one that I propose here. I'm really talking about the sense of ownership that people feel for something that they are passionate about because they helped to create it in some way. This sense of ownership is a big part of what makes an active community so special and interesting.

Too many companies think that they own the community with a level of ownership that includes exerting too much control over the people participating in the community. A better approach is to think of it this way: **the community "owns" the community**, and the employees of that company are an integral part of that community. Maybe this is just semantics, but I think it can help people think about the community in a way that facilitates collaboration and cooperation.

A company who starts a community is responsible for a few things. Clearly, they do own the infrastructure and the environment where the online community software resides. As a result, the company should feel a responsibility to maintain the software and keep it running well. The company is also responsible for facilitating the discussions and participating in the community along with the other community members. Finally, the company is also responsible for moderation and keeping people in check by deleting spam, porn and other content that is inappropriate for the community. As I've mentioned before, negative comments do not count as "inappropriate" for the sake of moderation.

If the company doesn't play nice with the community, the community will take their discussions elsewhere. Thinking about the issue of ownership in a way that encourages community members to consider themselves a real part of the community is just one more way to encourage people to remain actively engaged in the community.

Hosting On Domain or Off Domain

Should you host your new community on YourCompany.com or some other domain? It depends on the goals and objectives for your specific community and your situation. In most cases, you will probably want to host your community on your organization's domain; however, if you are building a community for your industry or a special project, it might make sense to host it on another domain. For example, eBay created the World of Good community on community.worldofgood.com as an

© 2009 Fast Wonder LLC

online marketplace focused on products that have a positive impact on people and the planet. Having it off domain helps distinguish it as a separate effort with different goals from other areas of the eBay website.

There are a few key differences between hosting on your domain or on another domain:

On Domain (YourCompany.com)

- More focus on your specific products. With a community on your domain, you can spend more time talking about your products without it feeling spammy.
- Clarity about who facilitates the community. When the community is hosted on yourcompany.com, it is obvious who is ultimately responsible for creating and maintaining the community while also facilitating the discussions in the community.
- Authority source for product info (features, etc.) When someone is looking for product specifications and lists of features, the company website is usually considered the authoritative source. This is also true for bug fixes and answers to questions about the product that can frequently be found in the community.

Off-Domain (YourIndustry.com, etc.)

- Focus on a broader segment or industry. With a separate domain, you might be able to focus the community on a much broader slice of the industry. This can be especially important if you are trying to drive the creation of a new industry or revitalization of an existing industry.
- Expect discussions about competitors. With this focus on a broader segment of the industry, people will discuss the entire industry, including your competition. You should be prepared to have open and honest discussions about the entire industry if you choose to host your community off-domain.
- Possibly a better perception of neutrality. You only get this benefit if you truly embrace the entire scope of your industry including allowing people to openly discuss competition along with your strengths and weaknesses as a company. If the community sees your company driving the community, then it is less likely that you will see this benefit.
- Slightly less authority about your products. Even when it is an employee talking about your products, it can be seen as less "official" since the discussion is happening off-domain.

Ultimately it comes down to your specific goals for the community and whether you think the community will be more successful on your site or on another domain. Like so many things in online communities, there is no right or wrong answer.

It comes down to a judgement call based on your specific situation.

Defining A Community Structure

It is important to keep in mind that every community software package is likely to have unique strengths and limitations when it comes to configuring your community. From a design and architecture perspective, I strongly recommend looking at this strengths and limitations of the platform and taking them into account before starting any design or architecture work. Make sure that any customizations that you do will be compatible with the community platform and will be easy to upgrade to future versions of the software. I have seen way too many companies try to shoe horn a design that just is not compatible with the platform they selected. In most cases, they are able to make it work for the initial launch, but then spend way too much time and effort during every upgrade or even worse, they get themselves into a situation where upgrading the platform or applying bug fixes becomes nearly impossible.

You should also take a careful look at how much structure to put in place when determining the category or discussion forum structure for your community. The specific categories will depend on the type of community and your specific situation, but I generally look at these three basic approaches: emergent, highly-structured, and adaptive.

Emergent

In an emergent structure, very few (if any) categories are defined before launch, and the structure is allowed to emerge based on the discussions that people are interested in having within your community. As the discussions unfold, you should start to see some common themes. New categories are created and discussions are placed into these categories based on the themes that are emerging in the community.

Advantages to the emergent approach.

- It is certainly the **easiest to implement** when creating a new community, since very little is defined before launch.
- **User buy-in** may also be higher, since the community members see themselves helping to create the structure by discussing topics relevant to their situation.
- You might also end up with something completely **unanticipated** that works very well, but is something that you never would have thought of creating as a category.

Disadvantages to the emergent approach.

- Community members may get **writer's block** when faced with an unstructured community. If confusion sets in and users can't figure out how to participate, they may never return to the community.
- A few early members may take the community so far **off-topic** that it becomes useless for the purpose that it was created to serve. While this is much less important for a social community, it can be devastating to a corporate community.
- It can be **more difficult to maintain** in the early days of the community, since you will need to rearrange posts into newly created categories.

I do not generally recommend an emergent structure for corporate communities; however, I could see it being useful in certain situations. In an environment where the industry or product was undefined or unclear and you wanted to avoid constraining people's ideas into categories allowing the structure to emerge might generate more innovative or unusual discussions. This structure is also more commonly and more effectively used in social (non-corporate) communities.

© 2009 Fast Wonder LLC

Highly Structured

In a highly structured community, all possible categories are defined before the community launch in great detail.

Advantages to the highly structured approach.
- The company creating the community has full **control** over the community structure with categories clearly defined in areas where people should focus their discussions.
- The community members have **clear expectations** about the types of conversations that are appropriate for the community.

Disadvantages to the highly structured approach.
- It is a **restrictive and inflexible** with fewer opportunities for the community to take the discussions into new areas.
- The company may also face more **community resistance**, since the community members did not have any input into the structure.
- The end result might also be a **structure that does not work** for the community with categories that do not resonate with the intended audience.
- Too many categories can also make the community seem very **fragmented** and give the appearance of less participation. This is particularly true if too many narrow categories are selected.

This structure may work fine in certain situations where the categories can be easily predicted and the environment is well understood; however, it can be a bit heavy handed. When it is used, I recommend sticking with broader categories rather than narrow ones whenever possible. Broad categories with more participation will make the community look much more active than if the same amount of participation is split among twice as many categories.

Adaptive

The adaptive approach is really a hybrid between the emergent and highly structured approaches. A few very broad categories are created to get the community started in the right direction, and additional categories are created as needed after people start participating.

Advantages of the adaptive approach.
- Better user **buy-in**, since the community members have some influence over the structure.
- The company maintains **some control** over the initial structure to help ensure that the discussions fulfill the purpose of the community.
- The community may also evolve in **unanticipated** positive directions that would not have been anticipated in advance.

Disadvantages of the adaptive approach.
- The company has a little **less control** over the structure.
- Getting **user traction** early in the process is required to help set the direction.

In most situations the adaptive approach is the one that I recommend. It is the most flexible, and it is fairly easy to implement.

Allowing Off Topic Discussions

When you create the structure for your community, you should assume that people will have some off topic discussions in your community. The best way to facilitate this without disrupting the rest of the community is to create a place where people can have these discussions. While they may be slightly off topic, I have found them quite productive for the community on occasion. For example, I've seen people using the community to find out which other members were planning to attend an upcoming conference on a related topic. As a community manager, I have used them to talk about interesting things going on in the company or the industry that did not directly relate to community. I caution against calling it something like "off topic", since people may take you up on the offer to discuss too many random topics. I've had pretty good luck calling it "the lounge" or something similar.

Ultimately, the structure you select for your community will depend on your individual situation. No one structure is right or wrong for every situation, so you may need to experiment a little to get it right for you. During the beta phase for your community, you can get quite a bit of feedback about the structure allowing for some adjustments prior to the public launch.

You should also plan to adjust the structure over time regardless of which approach you use. The industry and your products will change over time, and the community structure will need to evolve along with these changes.

Maintaining a Successful Corporate Community

The are many ways for a company to encourage or discourage participation in their community just by the way employees behave in the community, the way the community is facilitated, and how the infrastructure is maintained. There are a few things you can do to help ensure that the community is successful, while other activities are likely to drive the community away. This section will cover both the dos and don'ts along with some tips for maintaining a successful community.

What makes a community work

Being open and transparent. Being as open and transparent as possible will improve trust within the community. It often helps to explain the "why" behind some of your decisions to avoid being seen as closed or defensive. In general, people are more understanding, especially about difficult topics, if you can explain why the company responds in a certain way.

A company who listens (to good and bad). It is easy to listen and respond when people say nice things about you or your company, but you should also be responding when people complain or provide negative feedback. The key is to respond constructively with something helpful: a suggestion, information about upcoming changes, or just a simple thank you.

Actively engaged in the community. The company should not dominate the community, but they should be actively participating by creating new content, responding to feedback, and in general being visible in the community.

Encouraging new members. Whenever possible, welcome new members of the community, especially if they are particularly active in the community.

Making it easy for people to participate. Reduce the barriers to entry for people to participate and make it as easy as possible to join the community. Allowing people to view content before joining and a simple sign-up form with very few required fields can go a long way toward reducing the barriers to participation.

Integration into other relevant areas of the site. In most cases, it is simple to pull information from your community into static areas of your website. This makes your static website seem less static, and it drives more people to your community when they see a piece of content that they are interested in reading. For example, if you have a static page describing your efforts in sustainability, you could pull the 5 most recent blog posts or discussions from the sustainability section of your community into a sidebar on the static page.

What to avoid

Community as lip service. People can tell when a company creates a community to give the *appearance* of listening, while not really considering it a serious endeavor. If you aren't serious about engaging with your community, then you might be better off not spending the effort to create one.

Pushing marketing messages. When pushing marketing messages out to the community members takes precedence over two-way conversations and collaboration, you will start to see your community disappear. A community is about conversations between people, and you can talk about your products, but it should be done in a relevant and conversational tone, instead of sounding like a pitch or advertisement.

Deleting the negative. You should be responding to criticism, not deleting it. Again, communities are about conversation. If people feel like you are putting duct tape over their mouths when they express anything negative about the company, these people will simply post their negative comments somewhere else on the internet where it is likely more people will see the criticism and not hear your side of the story.

Barriers to collaboration. Community software, configuration, or policies can often create barriers to collaboration. Configure the software to make it easy for people to find content and sign up for the community. Your policies should create guidelines for use that help keep the community healthy without being so heavy handed that people aren't interested in participating. Flickr's community guidelines are a good example of how to write guidelines that are simple and even fun to read.

Neglected communities. Nobody wants to participate in a corporate community where no one in the company monitors or responds to questions or feedback. There are too many of these floating around the internet, so make sure that you have the resources to give your community care and feeding over the life of the community.

Dealing with the difficult

Every community has its fair share of difficulties. While you can never anticipate every difficult experience, many of them seem to fall into one of these four categories.

Negative Comments. As I mentioned earlier, do not delete negative feedback or negative comments. I generally hold off before responding to the negative feedback to see if other non-employee community members come to my rescue first. If not, you'll need to respond constructively and honestly with as much information as you are able to provide, and you need to respond without getting defensive.

Spammers. Spammers are a huge, painful thorn in a community manager's side. You should put aggressive, automated measures in place to deal with spam; however, also be prepared for them to find ways around your spam filters. Spammers are a creative group, and they will find ways to spam your community that you never thought was possible. Deal with the spam as quickly and completely as possible.

Pain in the ass. There are always those people who are just a pain. They complain that your documentation has a typo, you don't file bugs quickly enough, or anything else that isn't getting done to their exacting standards. In many cases, these are people who really do want to make things better. My advice in this case may sound counter-intuitive, but you should put them to work if possible and reward their efforts. If they complain about the documentation, see if you can convince them to re-write a section. If that works, you might find other ways to put them to work to channel that energy into fixing instead of complaining.

Don't feed the trolls. These are the people who complain and act out because they want attention. They will take up as much of your time as you give them in pointless arguments and distractions. It can be difficult for many people not to take the bait. Ignore them and resist the urge to give them the attention they crave. If they don't find someone to argue with, they will generally move on to another community where they can make trouble.

No community is perfect

You need to keep in mind that no community will ever be perfect: things will go wrong; your community software will have bugs; and people will get defensive or irate. In addition to the internal factors in the community, there are external influences that can creep into the community. Companies have PR nightmares that drive people into the community in droves to complain, but in great communities, the company responds effectively, addresses the issue, and works to resolve it quickly. When you have one of these crisis situations, keep the focus on summarizing and fixing, instead of blaming and justifying. Maintain open communication channels and deal with these imperfections and issues as quickly and openly as possible.

Promoting Your Community Efforts the Right Way

Now that we've talked about how to get started with an online community for your organization and how to successfully maintain it, we should spend some time on the right and wrong ways to promote your community efforts. Some of this advice also applies more broadly to promotion of other social media efforts as well.

Good ways to get the word out about your community

I wish there was an easy answer to the best way to get the word out about your community; however, it really comes down to basic marketing principles. Do your research to find your audience and talk about your community efforts in places that your target audience will see it. The specific methods you use to promote your community will depend on the type of community and the target audience. If your company already has an existing customer base, you should be using existing promotional vehicles to reach your customers. Look at the ways that you typically market your products, and include information about your community efforts in those promotions.

You should augment your traditional promotions with social media keeping the 'guiding principles' that I talked about earlier in mind. The key is to engage with social media on the community's terms with a focus on having a conversation *with* people, not a focus on pushing your messages *at* people. Talk openly and honestly about the new community on your corporate blog with information about why you launched it, what you hope to get out of it, and what you hope the members will get out of the community. People involved in the community effort can write personal blog entries or Twitter posts that talk specifically about their involvement in the new community. Audio or video podcasts might also be a good idea.

With any new community, always run a limited beta with your existing customers or a few potential customers if your company is still new. There are many benefits of running a beta. First, you can get their feedback and make improvements in the community before you launch. Second, you get a good base of initial content from people outside of the company, so that when you launch, it already looks like an active community. Third, these existing beta users can help promote the community by bringing in coworkers, friends, and others who might be interested in joining your community.

You might also consider providing small incentives for people to join and participate. You do not want people joining just to get the incentive and never coming back to participate, but some small incentive (t-shirt, etc.) can sometimes be a nice thank you gesture for signing up. Don't forget to make a special effort to find some way to reward the early beta participants after launch with special status, discounts, t-shirts, or something to say thank you.

Things to avoid when promoting your community

Do not promote your community on your competitor's sites. This is just slimy, and it will not be productive. The potential for backlash and negative publicity is not worth the one or two customers that you might pick up. It will also encourage your competitor to retaliate by promoting within your community.

Do not use social media (twitter, Facebook, blogs, etc.) with the sole purpose of pimping your products (go back to the 'guiding principles' section for more details). If you are already using social media, you should talk about your ideas, thoughts, and products with a personal spin (what YOU are doing as an individual in the new community).

Should you promote your products in the community?

The short answer is no, but it isn't really an absolute (yes / no) answer; it is really more of a continuum. Do not use your community to sell anything. Think of the community as way to generate awareness, not a place to close sales. Use your community to get people excited about your products: answer questions, talk about new features, and encourage people share stories about your product or company (customers and employees). If you can get people excited about your products, they will be motivated to figure out how to buy them.

Communities Fail Publicly

In the past, when you created a traditional web site, only your employees could tell how many people visited and interacted with your site. You could hide the dirty little secret that only 10 people per day visited your website, since only the employees with access to your analytics would ever know the truth. In other words, websites fail privately.

Online communities, on the other hand, fail publicly. When you launch an online community and nobody participates, you fail very publicly. Anyone visiting the community can see that people aren't participating, and it can be damaging to your brand.

Because communities fail publicly, it is important never to launch a community that is empty or nearly empty of content. You need to provide some content and set the tone for the community. It's like attending a party with a dance floor. If no one is dancing, it can be hard to get people started, but once you get a few people on the dance floor, others will take their lead and join in a similar fashion.

Here are a few quick summary tips to help make sure that your new community succeeds:

- Spend plenty of time in the planning phase to make sure that you have solid objectives, goals, and plan for how to launch a successful community.

- Have a content roadmap and plan for content. Participation takes work, and it won't magically happen without a little work on your part. The following section on community management covers this topic in more detail.

- Seed some content prior to launch. Create a few discussions with questions designed to stimulate conversations, and post other content that participants might find interesting.

- Run a beta with your favorite 10-25 people (depending on the size of the effort). These could friendly customers or people in your industry with interesting ideas.

- Promote your community and encourage your early beta testers to help get the word out about the community.

Spend the time during the planning phases of the community to make sure that you have a plan for the content and the resources to execute your plans over the long term. If you can't get the resources or don't have enough time to devote to the community, it might not be the right time to launch a community, and a static website might be a better choice for now.

Community Management

An online community manager will provide ongoing facilitation /
moderation, content creation, evangelism, and community
evolution to take your community to the next stage. In this
section, we'll talk about why community management is
important for any organization and some bad things that can
happen when you don't have a community manager (chaos,
spam, war). You would never launch a product without someone
in the product management position, and likewise, you should
never launch a community without a community manager.
Building a community is a big job, and it requires resources and
coordination to grow a successful community. The community
manager can be the person leading the charge to make sure
that the community is getting the attention it deserves.

© 2009 Fast Wonder LLC

Community Manager Role

Community managers frequently get asked this question, "What exactly do you do?" This question doesn't just come from friends and family; it also comes from customers, co-workers, and in the worst case from the management staff overseeing the community manager. Many community management tasks are behind the scenes and unpredictable, which can make it particularly difficult to understand exactly how community managers spend their days.

I see the online community manager role as having several key elements: ongoing facilitation, content creation, evangelism, community evolution, and monitoring. There are certainly many more tasks, but I suspect that 90% of the work falls into one of these five very broad categories.

Ongoing Facilitation

This is probably the activity that most people think of first. A community manager is an active participant within the community to answer questions, deal with trolls or other abuses, explain how things work, monitor the content closely, and much more. It also involves a lot of cat herding, since community managers frequently need to find ways to bring subject matter experts from around their company into the discussion to answer questions in an area where additional expertise is needed. It can also mean walking a very fine line between the community and the company by representing the company in community discussions and representing the needs of the community when working inside the company.

Content Creation

In any community, content needs to stay fresh and current regardless of whether you are talking about code releases for developer communities or other informational content relevant to your community members. People will wander away from a community that looks stale or inactive. This includes making sure that questions get answered (also part of facilitation), blogging, audio / video podcasts, or any other forms of content. The community manager should never be the sole content creator in any community, so this also involves convincing and encouraging co-workers and other general community members to create content in their areas of expertise.

Evangelism

Getting the word out about your community can take a number of forms depending on the type of community. In general this can be served by talking to people (customers and other interested parties), blogging, speaking at conferences, and being actively involved in related communities. The community manager should also be working closely with marketing to make sure that the community is being mentioned in other traditional marketing communications that are relevant to the types of people expected to join the community.

Community Evolution

This may be the most overlooked area for many communities. A good community manager will be looking into the future to come up with ways that the community should be changing and evolving along with your products, your industry, community platform technologies, and more. Any community can become stale and lifeless without enough thought going into improvements that will continue to keep the community engaged. New focus areas, community features, group activities / events and more should be planned.

Monitoring

While many discussions will take place in the community where you can easily find them and respond, the internet has many other places where people will talk about your company, community, products and more. Great community managers also monitor across many different sites to find and respond to conversations happening outside of the main community. See the section on monitoring dashboards for more details.

All of these items need to get an appropriate amount of attention, and you need to be careful not to put too much focus in any one portion of the community manager role. Responding to questions and writing an occasional blog post may not be enough if you want your community to flourish. Community management can be a tough job, but finding the right person to fill this role will help to ensure success in your community over the long term.

Skills Required for Community Managers

Now that we know more about the role of the community manager, this section focuses on the specific skills and traits that are required for an effective community manager. As I've mentioned before, the community manager role is very broad with every day being a little different, so the skills required are also very diverse. In general, the best community managers are the ones who seem to know a little bit of everything and have a knack for being able to figure out how to respond to new situations. Usually this comes from having a very broad and diverse background working in a number of different functions and industries throughout their career. Here are some of the skills and traits that I would look for in a community manager.

Patience

The community manager should not be the one responding to all of the questions. She needs to hold back and let others within the community participate. This is especially true when someone in the community is being particularly difficult. It can be easy to fire off an angry response that might be regretted later, but waiting until the emotions cool a bit can make the response more thoughtful and constructive. This includes patience with newbie community members. She may have heard the question a million times from other newbies, but this is probably the first time this particular person has asked the question. Taking a little time to welcome new community members while pointing them to a list of helpful resources (nicely) can go a long way toward helping to grow your community.

Networking

The best community managers are the ones who seem to know everyone and have a large group of colleagues that they can convince to help in various ways. These people do not typically acquire large networks by accident; they have good networking skills and are constantly meeting new people and growing their network.

Communication

Community managers should be great communicators. In some communities where the interactions are primarily online, good writing skills are essential. Public speaking skills are also be required for those community managers who also spend time organizing community events, evangelizing, and speaking at conferences on topics related to the community.

Facilitation

Community managers spend a fair amount of time making sure that the right people are involved and engaged in the community. No one person can (or should) respond to every

© 2009 Fast Wonder LLC

question or comment, so the community manager is frequently in the position of facilitating the discussions. The community manager should be able to facilitate discussions online making sure that a variety of people get a chance to participate while summarizing and communicating the decisions coming out of the discussion.

Technical Skills

Having at least a basic understanding of the technologies used in your community are important. This varies widely depending on the community, and not all community managers need to be highly technical. It certainly helps if the community manager is able to do some basic administration tasks without involving an administrator, especially for user account tasks like issues with passwords and profile information.

Marketing

For people managing developer communities, marketing may seem like a dirty word, but yes, marketing skills are a requirement for any community. The community manager needs to be able to promote community activities, solicit new members, and in general get the word out about the community. This probably involves doing some basic grassroots efforts while also working with the company's marketing team to get the community included in other communications.

Self Motivation

In most cases, no one will be looking over the community manager's shoulder telling him what to do. He needs to be self motivated to do whatever it takes to keep the community active and healthy without much direction from others.

Workaholic Tendencies

I do not mean that the community manager must work all the time; however, most communities do not exist in the 9-5 work hour schedule. People from all time zones participate at all hours of the day. Community managers probably want to at least check in on the community outside of business hours and respond to any hot topics or heated debates. This ties into the self motivation skills described above.

Organization

Community managers should also be organized. Keeping track of loose ends, making sure that questions are answered, being able to organize events, etc. all require good organizational skills and attention to detail.

Community Roles: Manager, Moderator, Administrator, and More

In many communities one person is responsible for all aspects of the community, and in most cases that person has some variant of the community manager title while also acting as moderator and administrator. In these cases, the community manager is directly responsible for the community, but they usually tap into a variety of resources throughout the company for help with moderation, management and administration as needed. A full time person responsible for moderation or administration of the software would be mostly bored and waiting for something to do in smaller communities, so it makes sense to use small portions of time from other team members.

However, in larger communities, there will often be entire teams of people with various roles within the community. Depending on the size of your community and your situation, you may need some or all of these roles. This section provides some ideas about how the roles can be divided for very large communities or within large companies.

Community Manager

This person is typically responsible for the overall strategy of the community in addition to managing all of the people in the roles below. Responsibility for the overall direction of the community includes: management of other team members, content plans, content creation, determining new functionality, and evolving the community.

Community Moderator

A moderator (or team of moderators) focuses on day to day responsibilities for the community: reading the threads, making sure that the right people are answering questions, moving threads when posted in the wrong place, dealing with spammers, and other day to day maintenance in the community.

Community Administrator

This person (or team) is responsible for the software and other technical aspects of the community (maintenance, upgrades, implementing new features, etc.)

Evangelist

In some very large communities, it might make sense to have a full-time evangelist who spends most of their time getting the word out about the community by presenting at conferences, attending user group meetings, and acting as the face of the community.

Hiring a Community Manager

Hiring a community manager can be tricky for companies, especially ones filling this position for the first time. As I've mentioned before, the community manager job itself can be a bit vague, like most leadership positions. The role changes from hour to hour depending on what happens in the community, and the person you hire will play a big part in shaping how your company engages with the outside world.

It is important to start by carefully defining your goals for the community along with what you want the new community manager to accomplish. Because this role is so different depending on the situation, what you should look for in a community manager also depends on your situation. You should be looking for someone with the skills required for your specific community needs. Most importantly, because the community manager frequently becomes the face of your organization within the community, you should be looking for someone who would do a great job of representing your company and who fits well within your corporate culture.

I also recommend spending some time looking at job descriptions that similar companies use for their community manager positions. There are a couple of job boards that focus on hiring community managers and related jobs. These should give you a feel for job descriptions, and they might also be good places to post your job description. Here are a few good community manager job boards:

- Web Strategy Job Board
- Community Guy Job Board
- ForumOne Jobs

The big question is "how much should I expect to pay this person?" In my experience, salary ranges for community managers vary widely. I've seen numbers ranging from less than $50,000 to over $150,000 a year for people in corporate community manager positions. I encourage you to read the Online Community Compensation Study from Forum One, which surveyed community managers and asked detailed questions about their current salary. Since the online community manager role is fairly new and not particularly well defined, salaries are all across the board with nothing like the traditional bell curve you would expect to see for salaries.

There are a large number of people making $150k and above; however, I expect that these people fall into two groups:

- people in higher level strategic positions in corporate environments who head a large organization responsible for the growth and management of multiple communities.
- community managers with name recognition or internet celebrity status working in high profile positions as community evangelists.

In general, community managers for technical communities (developers, etc.) tend to make more than end user, social communities. Salary also changes significantly depending on whether the role is really more low-end, tactical moderation or something more strategic, like building a new community or revitalizing a troubled community site. Job experience, scope, management responsibilities, location and how well known the person is can also make a big difference in the salary range as mentioned above.

Community Reporting Structures

There are many differences of opinion about where the community manager or the community team should fit into the reporting structure of any organization. In general, I think that it depends on the type of community. The community management function should report to the team most closely connected to the audience you are trying to serve.

Too many companies automatically put the community function under marketing, which works well for certain types of communities, but can be disastrous for other types of communities. For example, developer communities or customer support communities should rarely, if ever, report to marketing. However, I do think that marketing should manage the communities for certain types of customer communities or communities that support a certain marketing campaign. Communities focused on a specific product line could be driven out of a product marketing group.

Developer communities and open source communities should be driven out of a technology or engineering group, since developer and open source communities tend to work best when they are created by developers for developers. Developers in general have very little tolerance for marketing and anyone who lacks technical credibility.

Support communities should be driven as part of the broader support organization to ensure that the customers in the community are getting an appropriate level of support. The support staff deals with support questions all day and are the most appropriate group to be answering the questions in the support forums and making sure that support customers have what they need from the company.

In some cases, the community should report to the senior management within the organization. Some communities cover multiple functions including developers, support, customers, and product information. In those cases, the community team should be placed high enough in the organization to be able to effectively interface with all of the other teams in the organization. If the community is a critical part of the the products or services offered by the company, it might need to be it's own function within the organization.

It is worth spending some extra time deciding where the community function should be placed within the organization. You need to take a careful look at the audience for your

community and place the community in the appropriate
organization.

Motivation for Participating

We've talked about the benefits of having a community for the
company or organization; however, you also have to spend
plenty of time thinking about the benefits to the participants in
the community. It has to go both ways. A community will only be
successful if the participants and the organization both find
value in participating regularly in the community.

I have frequent conversations with people who are struggling
with whether or not to build an online community for a new
product, service, or website, especially when other, similar
communities already exist for the industry. Part of this
discussion often centers around why people would participate in
their community and what value would the members receive
that they were not already getting from other communities in
their industry or other social networks.

There are no easy answers to this question, and like many
questions about community management, the answer depends
on the situation; however, it boils down to a question of
motivation. What motivates people to participate in your
community?

I typically see some combination of these motivations:

- Status and Recognition
- Passion
- Work
- Developing Skills
- Career Advancement
- Learning
- Financial / Monetary
- Social
- Fun

The tricky part is that people are motivated in many different ways with complex interactions between motivations. For example, I might participate in a social media community as part of my work as a consultant because I think it will have long-term financial gain for me; however, I might be friends with many of the other members and participate for social reasons and because I have fun doing it while also feeling like I'm learning something.

Usually one of these motivations is the primary reason that a person comes into a community as a first time user. As a community manager or the organization sponsoring the community, you should focus on a couple of reasons that people might be motivated to participate and make them clear when you promote the community. Getting people motivated to visit the community for the first time is half of the battle.

© 2009 Fast Wonder LLC

It is also important to look at why people participate in your community and see how you can help get people more motivated to continue participating in the community over a significant period of time.

- Can you make it more fun? more social?
- What can you do to help people develop their skills and learn something new?
- How can you recognize the status of top contributors?
- Can you tap into their passion for a topic?

Online communities are complex endeavors. The people participating come from so many different places and backgrounds with different motivation for participating and different skills and information to contribute. Communities require planning and management over long periods of time to make them successful, but the benefits of participating in these communities can provide a tremendous value to the company when done right.

Advanced Topics

This chapter focuses on a few of the more advanced topics that you should consider when building a community. Most of these are optional, but strongly encouraged.

Monitoring Dashboards

I cannot put enough emphasis on the importance of using monitoring dashboards to understand what people are saying about you, your industry, your competitors and more. The information obtained can be used as ideas for blog posts, marketing messages, competitive analysis, product feedback and much more. In addition to providing inspiration, they also help you become more responsive to your customers by knowing when and where people are talking about your company and products. I usually include monitoring dashboards in my consulting proposals for anyone building a new community or trying to have a more effective social media presence through blogging or Twitter, since knowing what

© 2009 Fast Wonder LLC

people say about your company and your industry is such a critical element of community management, blogging, and other engagements with the community.

Who Should Use the Monitoring Dashboards

It is important to get as many people as possible within your company to use the monitoring dashboards. Each person or function within your company will notice or take action on different elements. As a community manager, I focus on people mentioning us on Twitter or in blogs. Product management and engineering might use the information to gather ideas for new features. Bloggers within the company can respond to what others are saying about your industry. Marketing can see how people are interpreting, misunderstanding, or resonating with the existing marketing messages.

The Format

The format really isn't that important from my perspective, since these monitoring dashboards can take a variety of forms all with the same content. Each person should be free to customize the dashboard and use whatever format is most natural for them. I'll briefly give a couple of examples of how they can be used to help you picture what they might look like for your company.

Quite a few people like to see it in a dashboard form, while other people who already live in their RSS reader would prefer to use their existing tools to monitor what people are saying about their company. In this case, you can maintain an OPML file that each person can import into an existing RSS reader.

Content is King

It is critical that you monitor the right types of content for your situation. In general, I think that most of the monitoring falls into 3 general buckets: vanity, industry and competition. I'll give some examples of what to monitor in each of these three areas along with some tools you might want to use; however, there are many different methods and sources to monitor with no way to ever cover all of them.

Vanity

- Blogs. Use feeds from Google Blog Search, Technorati or similar services to find people mentioning your products, your company, and key people within your company. You should also be using Google Blog Search to find people linking to your blog or websites using the link syntax (link:blog.yourdomain.com).
- Twitter. Even if you don't have a corporate Twitter account or actively use Twitter, I would still monitor what people are saying about you on Twitter.
- Depending on your company, you might also want to monitor what people are saying about you on other social sites: YouTube, Flickr, Delicious, FriendFeed, etc.

Industry

- Thought Leaders. Find at least the top 6-12 thought leaders within your industry and add their blogs to your monitoring dashboard. These people will have general insight into the industry and will provide ideas for future blog posts. You should also be following these people on twitter.
- Keywords. Use Google Blog Search or similar services to monitor keywords that apply to your industry to see what other bloggers are saying about your industry. These will need to fairly narrow words and phrases in order to filter out the noise, so pick something specific to track.
- Aggregation. Services like Techmeme can also be interesting ways to find the hot topics in your industry. I recently wrote a Techmeme Keyword Alert Pipe that can used to monitor keywords mentioned on Techmeme.

Competition

- Competitor Activity. Put the feeds from your top competitors blogs, news pages, job boards, Twitter, and anything else you can find with an rss feed in your monitoring dashboard to keep track of what they are saying about themselves.
- Support. If your competitors have public support sites (discussion boards, Get Satisfaction, etc.), you will want to track those, too.
- Keywords. Again, you'll probably want to track a few keywords (competitor names, products, etc.) to keep a pulse of what others are saying about your competitors.
- Individuals. Find a key employee or two from your top competitors who are very active on social websites. Add their twitter feeds, delicious bookmarks or other interesting information to your monitoring dashboards. At a previous job, I gathered a lot of very interesting information from the delicious feed of an employee at one of our competitors who liked to bookmark pages along with notes about how they could use the ideas to improve their product.

Getting Started

It really isn't as hard as it sounds. Chances are that you have people in your company who are already tracking some or all of this information. Now, you just need to find them and get them to share with the rest of you.

1. Send this list of the types of content you need around to your employees and have each of them gather a list of feeds that fall within these three categories.
2. Have someone very smart and insightful review these lists to pick out the ones that are most relevant and important. You can only track so much, so you are better off focusing on the important ones rather than trying to track everything.
3. Find someone with advanced knowledge of RSS who can use Yahoo Pipes or similar services to help filter some of the content and then create the dashboards or OPML file.
4. Distribute the monitoring dashboard to any employee who wants to use it. You may want to spend some quality time with the head of marketing, bloggers, and other key employees to make sure that they understand how to use the dashboard or OPML file.
5. Revisit the dashboard occasionally to update it with new information. For slow moving industries, you could probably update it once a quarter while others might need to update it every month.

© 2009 Fast Wonder LLC

This monitoring dashboard will be completely different for each company. Some will not care about certain types of content that I described above, while your industry may have very specific and unique items that will need to be monitored. Find the content that is right for you and your company, and find some way to monitor it.

© 2009 Fast Wonder LLC

Social Media Guidelines and Policies (Internal)

Does your company need a social media policy or guidelines for your employees? Maybe, maybe not.

In my experience, stringent rules and regulations encourage people to find ways to work around them. When companies come up with big lists of specific dos and don'ts, too many employees use them as an excuse to skirt the rules (well, they didn't say that I couldn't do x, y, z).

Broad guidelines based on good practices might be a better way to go. When I worked at Intel, we frequently had ethics training, and I remember an instructor saying that most things could be decided by thinking about the following 2 questions:

- Would I want my mother to know that I did this?
- Would I be embarrassed if I read about it on the front page of the Wall Street Journal?

Social media policies of the rules and regulations variety are not the best way to encourage participation in social media sites. Instead, I recommend focusing on broader social media guidelines for your employees. The guidelines should cover blogging, podcasting, comments, Facebook, Twitter, and other social sites. I would keep the list of guidelines short and broad with a focus on helping employees participate in social media rather than restricting them to a list of "approved" activities. Again, this is not intended to be a list of rules and regulations.

Here are a few things you may want to include in your company's social media guidelines for participation:

- Be authentic, honest and conversational in your posts. Leave the marketing speak and press release format for other parts of the website.
- Use good judgment about content and be careful not to include confidential information about your company, customers, or vendors.
- Listen to people and respond to as many comments as possible with constructive feedback. Allow negative comments (delete the spam) - the key to managing comments is to respond rather than censor. Avoid getting defensive and ignore the trolls where appropriate.
- When you talk about your company or competitors, do so under your real name making your alliance with your company clear (no company wants a repeat of the Whole Foods message board fiasco). If you are providing your opinion, it is also a good idea to make sure people know that you are giving your opinion.
- Peer reviews, especially for lengthy or complicated posts, should be encouraged, but not required. It's always nice to have someone double check grammar and technical details before it goes out to the world.
- Personal blogs for employees should be encouraged. They are a great way to show the world that you hire smart, interesting people.

© 2009 Fast Wonder LLC

A few things that you might not want to include in your social media policy:

- Lengthy approval processes for content. They not only stifle creativity and spontaneity, but they can also render many posts obsolete. Social media often requires quick, short responses to questions, trends, and issues. You want your employees to be involved in those discussions as they happen, not days or even hours later.
- Restrictions about who is allowed to participate and who is not. Assuming that you hire great people, you should be able to provide employees with guidelines to participate and trust them to do the right thing. If someone isn't playing nicely with others online, it should be addressed as part of a broader performance management plan with that specific employee.

This is not meant to be an exhaustive list, and it probably wouldn't work for every company; however, I do think it provides an interesting starting point and approach for working with employees to help them participate in social media (rather than restricting them from participating).

Community Guidelines (External)

While internal social media guidelines for employees are optional, I consider community guidelines for members mandatory. It is important for your community members to know what is and what is not acceptable behavior within your online community. When you have a community member who is participating in a manner that isn't appropriate, you can give her a warning and point her to the community guidelines for more details and then remove her from the community if the behavior continues. If you don't have community guidelines, people don't know how to behave and any removal of members will seem arbitrary. However, this doesn't mean that the guidelines can't be fun and interesting.

First, separate the community guidelines from your terms and conditions. Nobody reads the terms and conditions, except for the lawyers, and they are generally written in a way to cover the company's assets but not in a way that make them easy to understand for users.

Create community guidelines that are short, simple and fun to read. The best way to illustrate what I mean is through a few examples.
- Digg: "Would you talk to your mom or neighbor like that?"
- Flickr: "Don't be creepy. You know the guy. Don't be that guy."

Here's one more example of some community guidelines that I wrote for Shizzow: "Being creepy or stalking people does not make a good impression, and it is not a good way to meet new people."

Save the legal language for the terms and conditions and take the time to have a little fun with your online community guidelines.

© 2009 Fast Wonder LLC

Reputation Systems

When I talk about reputation systems (or a reputation engine), I am referring to ways to award points or some other status measure to community members as a "reward" for participating. Many community platforms have a reputation system built into the application to automatically award points for posting discussions, blogs, wiki documents, correctly answering questions, and other community activities. The points accumulated by users probably show up in some way on the users' profiles.

The Good

People like getting points and being recognized for their contributions within a community. It encourages participation and keeps people motivated to participate in the community. Community managers can use the reputations to highlight and reward key members with additional access (moderation access, etc.) or with other rewards like t-shirts.

The Bad

People will figure out how your system works, and they will find creative ways to game it. Maybe they respond to posts with trivial answers or post discussions with content of little value solely to gain points. This is especially true in technical communities where people will game it just for the challenge. This leads many people to claim that reputation systems are worthless and should never be used.

The Practical

It doesn't have to be an "all or nothing" approach. I think that there is a middle ground where carefully configured reputation systems can be useful.

I suggest putting the responsibility on other community members to award points to their peers for quality posts. One way to accomplish this is by configuring your reputation system to put a heavy weight on correct / helpful answers with little or no points awarded for quantity of posts.

Do not be afraid to adjust the weights over time when you see abuses. You can start out with points awarded for starting discussions, but if you see users posting just to get points, reconfigure it and be clear with your community that you reconfigured it and why. Sometimes communities can be good at self-policing members with bad behavior.

Also make sure that people can easily scan the posts of other users. If I see a user with a bunch of points, I should be able to go to the profile and see whether they have good, quality answers or just meaningless quantity. Community members are smart, and they will be able to tell which community members are participating in meaningful ways as long as you give them the tools to do it.

I also advise against automating rewards based on points. I might be willing to automate for something small like a t-shirt, but not for anything meaningful like moderation permissions, commit rights in open source, or anything else of value.

This is just a starting point. There are many, many ways to measure the reputation of community members and to use it for rewards based on contributions.

Rewarding Community Members

I spend quite a bit of time talking with clients about incentives and rewards for participation in their community, especially when they are launching new communities. Ultimately, the participation in the community should provide enough benefits that members will want to continue to participate as it's own reward. I offer quite a few cautions against offering monetary incentives, because in my past experience, they tend not to be effective. This is especially true for communities where the members are technologists, since people working in the technology industry are already well compensated in most cases.

However, I hadn't really spent much time thinking about the psychology behind it until I read a particularly interesting short post by Richard Millington. He suggests sending them a fruit basket or some other surprise gift as a thank you for their participation. When you use money as a reward, it starts to feel like work, and your monetary rewards are likely to be much lower than what the person would "earn" for other work resulting in resentment and lowered enthusiasm for the community.

The point here isn't that a fruit basket is the right reward for excellent community participation, but a little bit of creativity goes a long way toward finding interesting ways to reward participants while staying away from monetary rewards. What kind of small gifts can you send people to say thank you for doing something nice? These gifts can be as small as a pack of M&Ms. What is something exclusive that you can offer someone as a reward that they can't get elsewhere? I know one person who often wears a t-shirt that is only given to people with commit status for this particular open source project. He's proud of having special status within the community. You should think of ways that you can reward people with special status in your community that will make them proud of having achieved it. A special t-shirt or other ways for them to display this special status can help reinforce this reward.

Start with building the community in a way that members get intrinsic benefits just for participating. Use thank you gifts to augment the other benefits that people get for participating, but stay away from monetary rewards.

Importance of Place and Context in Online Communities

I realized something very interesting about my computer usage patterns a while ago. For most tasks, I use the GUI environment on my Mac, since I mostly live in my web browser, instant messaging, Twitter apps, and RSS reader for blog posts. However, my background as a sys admin takes over whenever I am doing certain tasks, despite the fact that I haven't been a sys admin since the mid-1990s. I found that I shift to the command line automatically for any tasks that I associate with Unix. For example, to edit any configuration file, I'll go to the terminal window and use vi without even considering editing it using the various text editors that I would use to edit almost any other file on my hard drive. It suddenly dawned on me that context plays a very significant role in my computer usage.

When I talk about "context" throughout the rest of this section, I'm referring to the set of circumstances or facts that surround a particular event or situation. Bear with me, I am going somewhere relevant with this discussion after one more minor diversion. I was talking to Amber Case a few weeks ago about the role that context plays in human memory. We tend to recall past memories more accurately if we are in the place where we first heard them or in a similar context. I started thinking about the role of context in my strange computer usage patterns. In a context that I associate with Unix or sys admin tasks, I revert to the command line without a second thought even for tasks that could be done as easily using a GUI tool.

I started wondering and thinking about the role that context plays in our social behavior as we interact in online communities and social networks. These online communities and social networks are the location or place equivalents of the local pub, coffee shop, library, or university, but in a specific online context. They are the places where we hang out (virtually) with friends, colleagues, family, and even strangers with common interests. We use our online communities and social networks to learn new things, gather information, and keep up with news about the other people in our lives. These are the new places that become the context for our interaction with people online.

I have noticed that I tend to behave and interact in very different ways depending on the community or social network that I am using. My interactions on Facebook, Twitter, and LinkedIn are very different. I use Twitter for conversations and sharing information with people; Facebook for finding non-work information about my friends, and LinkedIn for finding work-related information. Realistically, I could send people messages using any of those social networks, but I tend to use Twitter to send messages to people and engage people in conversations; however, I have friends who would say that they primarily use Facebook to engage in conversations. I suspect that all of this comes back to context. We each associate certain activities with our personal context for that situation.

OK, so this is an interesting abstract topic, but what does all of this really mean? For anyone tasked with building online communities for your organization, you need to focus on creating a sense of place, like the neighborhood coffee shop, where people want to hang out and chat with other people who have common interests. Spend some time thinking about how to create an environment focused on discussions and connections between people. Provide other relevant information for your community members, but keep the community as focused as possible on the people and discussions that facilitate connections and interactions between those people. Let your community members develop a sense of place in your community and with it a meaningful context for their interactions within your community.

© 2009 Fast Wonder LLC

Future of Corporate Communities

Corporate communities and social communities have frequently had very different ideas and norms for behavior; however, there have been some recent trends toward bringing the two closer together. As people increasingly use social networks for personal interactions, they are starting to expect to see similar features and functionality in their corporate communities.

Enterprise community platforms (SocialText, Clearspace and others) are starting to shift the focus more toward people with the addition of social networking, ad hoc groups, and conversation functionality leading the way. These features are just a couple of examples of how community software focused on the enterprise is incorporating the features that people have been using extensively in their personal online community interactions through sites like Facebook, Twitter, and more to connect with other people.

If you look at the early community software platforms and other early ways of building communities (mailing lists, etc.), the focus was on the data more than the person. Inside companies, the focus was similar. Companies had knowledge bases, document repositories, email and other ways for people to share data. Most of these applications made it easy to find data, but difficult to find out any real information about the people behind the data. Even some of the applications designed to help coworkers find other people within the company were often skill based, which made it easy to find someone with Java programming expertise but not the sort of information that tells you about the person behind the skill set.

I always talk about how communities are all about the people. This has always been an important concept, but it has been more true in social communities and less true in many corporate communities. Recently, I have been seeing a bigger trend toward companies and other organizations putting the focus on the people in corporate communities. The information is still important, but I like seeing this shift toward people. Knowing more about the person behind the data can help put the data into context. For example, information about venture capital investments coming from Dawn Foster would be less credible than information about venture capital from Guy Kawasaki.

Having the functionality to connect with other people in a corporate community, whether it is an internal company community or an external community focused on a company's products, helps us strengthen our connections with other people who share similar interests. This trend toward putting the focus on people is an important step in the right direction for corporate communities.

About the Author

Dawn Foster is a consultant, community manager, event organizer, blogger, podcaster, technology enthusiast and business professional. She provides consulting services for companies wanting to engage with online communities and has more than 13 years of experience in business and technology with expertise in strategic planning, management, market research, social media, blogging, podcasting, rss, community building, web 2.0, and open source software.

Dawn regularly blogs about online communities as the author of the Fast Wonder Blog, and she blogs for GigaOM's WebWorkerDaily. She is the community evangelist for Shizzow, a co-founder of Legion of Tech and is an organizer for the Portland BarCamp and Ignite Portland events.

Dawn holds an MBA from Ashland University and a bachelor's degree in computer science from Kent State University.

© 2009 Fast Wonder LLC

Previously, she worked at Intel, Jive Software, Compiere, and a Midwestern manufacturing company in positions ranging from Unix system administrator to market researcher to community manager to open source strategist.

You can read Dawn's Fast Wonder Blog to learn more about her ideas: fastwonderblog.com

Additional Resources

More content by Dawn M. Foster

Fast Wonder Blog
Many articles on topics related to online communities, social media, and more.
http://fastwonderblog.com/

Starting Point
Starting point for new readers with links to top posts.
http://fastwonderblog.com/starting-point/

Yahoo Pipes and RSS Hacks
Learn how to create and use Yahoo Pipes and related tools for more effective RSS usage.
http://fastwonderblog.com/yahoo-pipes-and-rss-hacks/

© 2009 Fast Wonder LLC

Fast Wonder Consulting Services

Online Community Building
- Building a community around your products
- Managing communities
- Open source communities
- Assistance with interviewing and hiring a community manager

Social Media
- Blogging strategy and implementation guidance
- Social networking presence (Facebook, Twitter, etc.)

Information Monitoring and Industry Intelligence
- Using various RSS tools and Monitoring Dashboards to monitor what people are saying about you, your company, competitors, and the industry.

Training and Speaking
- Customized training for employees on a variety of community engagement and social media topics.
- Speaking engagements.

Presentations

- Companies and Communities: Participating without being sleazy.
- Online Communities: short and basic introduction to online communities
- Online Communities and Marketing: comprehensive 40+ slides on how people in marketing can engage with online communities.
- Open Source Communities: overview of how open source communities function
- What Would Dr. Seuss Say about Online Communities: fun with online communities presented in Ignite style (slides with audio included in this link).
- Online Community Manager: Yes, it's really a job: careers in community management.
- Social Media Training: short training session about social media
- Online Community Training: training session for people getting ready to build online communities.

These presentations and more can be found at:
http://fastwonderblog.com/speaking/

© 2009 Fast Wonder LLC

Information about online communities from other sources

- http://www.web-strategist.com/blog
- http://www.onlinecommunityreport.com/
- http://conniebensen.com/blog
- http://www.communityguy.com
- http://www.feverbee.com/

Find Dawn M. Foster on various social media sites

- **Twitter:**
  http://twitter.com/geekygirldawn
- **Facebook:**
  http://www.facebook.com/profile.php?id=500062544
- **FriendFeed:**
  http://friendfeed.com/geekygirldawn
- **LinkedIn:**
  http://www.linkedin.com/in/dawnfoster
- **Delicious:**
  http://delicious.com/geekygirl
- **ClaimID:**
  http://claimid.com/dawnfoster
- **Shizzow:**
  http://www.shizzow.com/people/geekygirldawn
- **Upcoming:**
  http://upcoming.yahoo.com/user/92824/

Feedback

I would love to hear your feedback about this book. Please let me know what you liked or didn't like, send suggestions for improvement, point out typos and more!

Contact Information

The best way to contact Dawn M. Foster at Fast Wonder: dawn@fastwonder.com

Fast Wonder LLC
4110 SE Hawthorne #131
Portland, OR 97214
503-702-7223

www.ingramcontent.com/pod-product-compliance
Lightning Source LLC
Chambersburg PA
CBHW071219050326

40689CB00011B/2369